SHORELAND TREES

WEEPING WILLOW

PUSSY WILLOW

MAPLE

PINE

BALDCYPRESS

POPLAR

NOTE: TREE SHAPES SHOWN LEAFLESS.

ALDER

COTTONWOOD

THIS
NATURE NOTEBOOK
BELONGS TO:

_____

_____

_____

WATER
HICKORY

SUM,

RIVER BIRCH

WATER OAK

NOTE: TREES SHOWN IN SIZE PROPORTION
TO ONE ANOTHER.

Library of Congress Cataloging-in-Publication Data
Arnosky, Jim.
Shore walker / by Jim Arnosky.
p.   cm. — (Jim Arnosky's nature notebooks)
SUMMARY: Presents tips on observing plant and animal life along the
seashore, with blank pages provided for keeping records.
ISBN 0-679-86718-X
1. Seashore ecology—Juvenile literature.
2. Seashore—Juvenile literature.
[1. Seashore.   2. Nature study.]   I. Title.   II. Series: Arnosky, Jim.
Jim Arnosky's nature notebooks.
QH541.S33A77   1997   574.5'2638'0723—dc20   96-21648

Printed in the United States of America   10 9 8 7 6 5 4 3 2 1

SHORE WALKER

Random House New York

SHORE WALKER

If, like me, you are drawn to water and enjoy nothing better than walking along a shoreline, if you love looking for shells, rounded stones, and footprints pressed in wet sand—then you are a shore walker through and through. Wherever water—salt or fresh—meets land, things get interesting.

TROUT AND MAYFLY

SHORELAND IS THE END
OF THE WORLD FOR
TERRESTRIAL CREATURES,
AND A SHORELINE MARKS
THE BEGINNING OF THE
MYSTERIOUS UNDERWORLD
OF AQUATIC LIFE.

SANDPIPER

TYPES OF SHORE

Shoreland can be as rugged as a rocky coast or as smooth and accessible as a sandy beach. It can be clearly defined, like pond water lapping against mud banks. Or it can be a subtle change, like that from open water to marsh to high, dry land.

The shore walker has a variety of places to explore: pebbled, sandy, rocky, weedy, soggy shore and more.

THE ROCKY NEW ENGLAND SEA-COAST IS FAMOUS FOR ITS RUGGED CHARACTER, BUT...

CAUTION: ROCKY SHORES SUCH AS THIS ARE BEST OBSERVED WITH BINOCULARS FROM A SAFE DISTANCE ON FIRM, WELL-TRAVELED PATHS!

... FROM THE SMOOTH, ROUNDED BOULDERS ON A RIVERFRONT,

A SECLUDED WOODED LAKESHORE,

TO THE GREAT GRASSY DUNES ON A SANDY OCEAN BEACH,

EACH AND EVERY SHORELINE HAS ITS OWN UNIQUE CHARACTER.

9

PLANT SUCCESSION

On shores that gradually change first to marsh then to drier land, you may notice a pattern to the plants: low aquatic plants to taller plants; lilies to reeds to arrowheads to cattails; and beyond the cattails, water-loving willows or alders. The best way to see this is not from the shore but from the

5) WOODY PLANTS

PLANT
SUCCESSION
AS SEEN FROM
WATER.

4) CATTAILS

3) ARROWHEADS

2) REEDS

1) WATER LILIES

water, while wading slowly in the shallows. Once you understand basic shoreline plant successions, you will be better able to record your shore sighting in your notes. And sketching shorelines in your notebook will become easier.

SHORE PATH

SIDE VIEW

SHORE WILDLIFE

Water attracts wildlife. Even the most shy forest creatures come to shorelines to drink or hunt for food in the soft soil and shallow water.

SHORE WALKERS ENJOY THE GREATEST VARIETY OF BIRDS~ FROM PERCHERS TO WADERS TO SWIMMERS.

GREATER YELLOWLEGS

VED-BILLED GREBE

UDDY TURNSTONE

YELLOWTHROAT WARBLER

A RACCOON FEELING
AROUND FOR CRAYFISH

Frogs, salamanders, water snakes, and
turtles all live along shorelines. In
water only inches deep, fish can be
seen chasing frogs or aquatic insects.

Shore walkers are bird watchers, bug
hunters, *and* animal trackers.

BULLFROG

DAMSELFLY

SPOTTED
SALAMANDER

SHORE WALKING SAFETY

As always in the Great Outdoors, be careful where you step. Thoroughly test soft-looking shoreland with a stick to make sure you won't sink in when walking. When wading in very shallow water, make sure every step is on firm bottom. Along the seashore, be aware of tidal changes.

If you happen to be where poisonous snakes are known to live, avoid walking right along the water's edge. That is where snakes sun

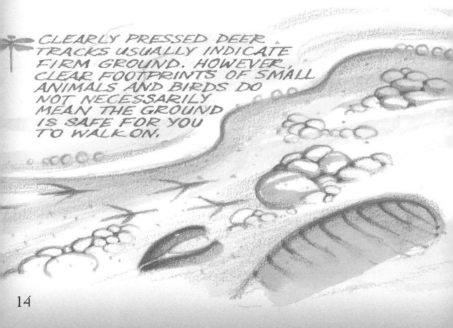

CLEARLY PRESSED DEER TRACKS USUALLY INDICATE FIRM GROUND. HOWEVER, CLEAR FOOTPRINTS OF SMALL ANIMALS AND BIRDS DO NOT NECESSARILY MEAN THE GROUND IS SAFE FOR YOU TO WALK ON.

themselves or wait coiled to strike at water-loving prey. Many common water snakes, though non-poisonous, are not harmless. They are high-strung and may bite when alarmed or cornered.

And if you live in alligator country, never, *never* walk where you cannot see everything that is on the ground for at least 20 feet all around you.

RECORDING FINDINGS

When you are recording a special find or simply noting the pleasure of a day along the shore, begin with the date and time, a comment on the weather, and the name of the body of water on whose shore you are walking. Choose your words carefully to describe exactly what it is like where you are. Tell how warm or cold the air feels. Mention the color of the water. Note the sounds of water, insects, birds, and frogs. Make small sketches of anything and everything you find interesting—piles of stones, insects, plants. Use rulers, boxes, and circles to highlight or separate one section of your notes from the rest. If you mention a species of wildlife, include a small drawing of the animal you saw. If you see something unusual, register your wonder and excitement with exclamation points! It's okay to sketch in little self-portraits. I often do.

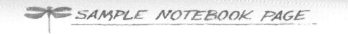

OCT. 23, 1994

CRINKLE COVE
WATER CALM, AIR WARM.

LATE THIS EVENING, WHILE WALKING
ALONG THE SHORE, I SPOTTED AN
UNUSUAL FISH FOR OUR COVE.
IT WAS A WARMOUTH.

THE FISH WAS
VERY CLOSE TO SHORE

WARMOUTH

HERE ARE SOME OTHER THINGS I SAW.

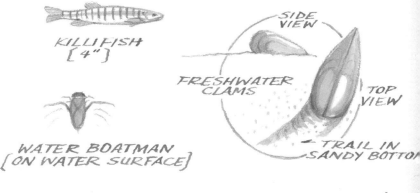

KILLIFISH
[4"]

FRESHWATER
CLAMS

SIDE
VIEW

TOP
VIEW

WATER BOATMAN
[ON WATER SURFACE]

TRAIL IN
SANDY BOTTOM

ALL THIS IN WATER ONLY INCHES DEEP!

17

YOUR NATURE NOTEBOOK

Your nature notebook is small and flexible so you can roll it up, put it in a pocket, and carry it wherever you go. But as small as it may be, it can hold many wonderful experiences. Take care to write small and fit a lot on every page. Be careful in the hot sun. Wear sunblock, especially on your nose and cheeks. Sun reflecting off the water can burn you badly. If the shoreline is grassy or weedy, check yourself occasionally for ticks.

I'll be dropping in on a few more pages throughout the rest of the book to tell you a little more about life along the water's edge. Until then…

HAPPY SHORE WALKING!

Jim Arnosky

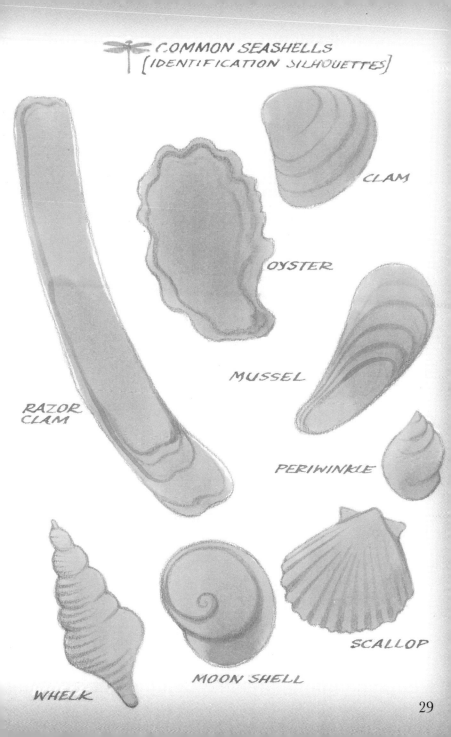

COMMON SEASHELLS
[IDENTIFICATION SILHOUETTES]

CLAM

OYSTER

MUSSEL

RAZOR
CLAM

PERIWINKLE

SCALLOP

WHELK

MOON SHELL

29

MANY INLAND WATERS WERE ONCE PART OF
A SALTWATER SEA, EVIDENCE OF THIS CAN
BE FOUND IN RANDOM SHORELINE STONES
CONTAINING FASCINATING FOSSIL FORMS
OF LONG~GONE SEA CREATURES.

SEASHELL FOSSILS

TRILOBITES
[EXTINCT MARINE
ARTHROPODS]

ENTIRE FISH FOSSIL~A RARE FIND!

UNDERWATER PLANTS

ON SHORES WHERE YOU CAN SEE DOWN
INTO WATER AT LEAST ONE FOOT DEEP,
LOOK FOR THESE COMMON FRESHWATER
SUBMERGED PLANTS.

THREE KINDS OF WATER CABBAGES

WATER MILFOIL

COONTAIL

EELGRASS

53

ABOUT THE AUTHOR

Naturalist Jim Arnosky has written and illustrated over 35 nature books for children. His titles have earned numerous honors, including American Library Association Notable Book Awards and Outstanding Science Books for Children Awards presented by the National Science Teachers Association Children's Book Council Joint Committee. He has also received the Eva L. Gordon Award for Body of Work for his contribution to children's literature.

An all-around nature lover, Mr. Arnosky can often be found fishing, hiking, boating, or videotaping wildlife on safari. He lives with his family in South Ryegate, Vermont.

SHORELAND PLANTS

GOLDENROD

FIREWEED

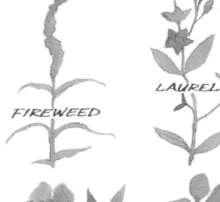

LAUREL

BLUE FLAG

SWAMP ROSE

HIBISCUS

SKUNK CABBAGE

PITCHER PLANT

ROYAL
FERN

CINNAMON
FERN

WILD
PINE